GW01459803

Original title:
Fragrant Free Verse

Author: Giselle Montgomery
ISBN HARDBACK: 978-1-80566-772-8
ISBN PAPERBACK: 978-1-80566-842-8

The Scent of Moonlit Memories

Under the stars, a flower sneezes,
Petals flutter like giggling breezes.
An owl hoots, thinking he's wise,
But the moon just smirks with surprise.

A cat in a hat strolls by with style,
Paws tapping softly, oh what a while!
The night whispers secrets, quirky and sweet,
While shadows dance on their silent feet.

A breeze carries jokes from a nearby tree,
Where squirrels are jesters, feeling quite free.
They plan a parade with acorn crowns,
As the night giggles, without any frowns.

Dandelions puff out their heads in glee,
Blowing wishes to the moon and to me.
With every chuckle, the world fades away,
In this aromatic night where we all want to play.

The Bouquet of Lost Memories

In a vase of chaos, I find
Lilies dancing, yet they remind,
Of socks misplaced in the wash, oh dear,
And the dog's breath, reeking of cheer.

Petunias shout misplaced jokes,
While daisies giggle at sneaky folks.
Oh, bouquet, a comedy show,
Of sniff and snort—what a flow!

Olfactory Memories Untangle

The scent of toast burns in the air,
Recalling mornings without despair,
Where pancakes flew for a sugary kiss,
And syrup landed, oh what a bliss!

Basil whispers past mischief, loud,
Like that time I danced for a crowd,
But tripped on air, a glorious fall,
Leaving laughter lingering, that's all.

Gossamer Threads of Fragrance

A web of scents, a clown's parade,
With cotton candy and lemonade,
The roses tease with their cheeky laugh,
As I trip over my own daft path.

Minty fresh, a prankster's breath,
Sneaking up with cheeky stealth,
While lavender giggles, soft and sweet,
An olfactory jest, oh what a treat!

Unraveled Blooms of Emotion

Each petal whispers, 'Do not fret,'
As memories bloom, I can't forget,
The marshmallow fight, oh what a sight,
With maybe the cat, mid-air, took flight.

Chrysanthemums fuel silly dreams,
Of absurd antics and ice cream streams,
Unraveled blooms, each sigh a jest,
In this garden, we laugh the best.

Beneath the Aroma of Adventure

Beneath the spice of whimsy's charm,
Curious noses sniff the farm.
A cabbage hat, a pickle shoe,
Who knew veggies could giggle too?

With every step, a scenty dance,
Bananas wear a yellow pants.
A riddle in a raspberry's hue,
Even carrots laugh when they chew.

Lingering Scent of a Sunlit Day

A splash of sunshine on the nose,
Honey bees in tiny prose.
Lemonade spills, a fizzy affair,
Sipping laughter fills the air.

Prancing pineapples in the breeze,
Chasing giggles, tickling trees.
Cotton candy clouds float by,
While chocolate dreams begin to fly.

Enchanted by Floral Muse

Daisies dance in funny hats,
With twirling bees that speak like chats.
A daffodil drops a silly rhyme,
While tulips giggle, keeping time.

Butterflies wear polka dots,
Sharing jokes in sunny spots.
A garden party, wild and grand,
With flower crowns and jester's band.

Mellow Hues of Spring's Breath

A gentle breeze speaks soft and low,
Carrot tops in rowboat show.
With clowns on greens, who knows the score?
A cabbage pie—who could want more?

Each petal whispers jokes so bright,
Tickle the tulips, what a sight!
While dainty frogs make quite the fuss,
In puddles laughing, just like us.

The Spice of Life's Journey

Life's a mix of herbs and zest,
Bumping spices, we are blessed.
Chili laughs and pepper grins,
Add some garlic, let fun begin!

Tacos dancing in the sun,
Salsa twirls, oh what a run!
Laughter sizzles in the pan,
Spiced-up dreams of every plan.

The Dance of Scented Shadows

In the kitchen, shadows play,
Oregano leads the ballet.
Cinnamon spins with a wink,
While basil bursts—it's time to think!

Garlic hops, a funky beat,
As thyme reels on happy feet.
Flavors prance in cheeky glee,
Scented shadows, wild and free!

Unfolding Petals in Harmony

Petals giggle as they bloom,
Rose and lav'nder clear the gloom.
Daisy's dance, a gentle sway,
While clovers cheer and laugh away.

Jasmine whispers sweet surprise,
Sunflowers wink with golden eyes.
They spin tales in fragrant rhyme,
Enjoying every silly time.

The Aroma of Untold Stories

Baking cookies, tales unfold,
With chocolate chips, just pure gold.
Each whiff a giggle, air of fun,
What mischief have we just begun?

Brownies chuckle, pies sing loud,
Cinnamon rolls feel quite proud.
In every bite, a story lurks,
With each aroma, joyworks!

Fragrance Beyond the Surface

In the garden, smells collide,
Petunias whisper, daisies slide.
A rose sneezes, pollen flies,
While tulips chuckle 'What a surprise!'

Lavender leans, a bit too bold,
Sharing secrets, both sweet and old.
Chives giggle, fresh and spry,
While sunflowers wink at the buzzing sky.

The Secret Language of Scented Ferns

Ferns dance lightly in the breeze,
Their laughter tickles, if you please.
A minty joke? They might just tell!
While daisies laugh, in secret dwell.

Grass tickles toes, as squirrels prance,
Each whiff a new, unexpected chance.
The wild thyme guffaws, all can hear,
As a rose rolls its eyes, 'Oh dear!'

Conversations with Nature's Breath

Breezes chat with flowers bright,
Jasmine giggles, feeling light.
A dandelion bursts with glee,
While violets play hide and seek, you see.

The oak tree whispers tales so grand,
While petals flutter, hand in hand.
A bumblebee buzzes in delight,
With laughter echoing through the night.

A Journey Through Botanical Skies

Clouds wear perfume, soft and sweet,
As lilacs prance with playful feet.
The wind's a jester, swirling round,
While fresh thyme sings, a funny sound.

Cacti chuckle, spiky and sly,
With a giggle, they reach for the sky.
The sunset bows, a fragrant muse,
As night blooms in a laughing fuse.

Breath of Blossoms and Thoughts

In the garden, thoughts collide,
Silly blooms in laughter hide.
Daffodils wear shoes of green,
As bees dance like they're on a screen.

Petunias gossip, tulips giggle,
As restless ants begin to wiggle.
The sun, a jester in the sky,
Winks at flowers passing by.

Breezes tease the daisies fair,
Whispering secrets in the air.
Each scent a riddle, smiles galore,
Who knew flowers could be such a chore?

In this patch of pure delight,
Even thorns bring a funny bite.
So sniff away, feel the cheer,
Especially when the roses leer.

The Essence of Wind and Wonder

A breeze too bold, a gust too brash,
Tickling leaves, causing quite the clash.
Laughter floats on currents free,
As clouds wear hats of cotton candy.

Merry winds blow through the trees,
Combing branches with gusty ease.
Sprinkling joy like fancy confetti,
Turning serious folks into confet-ty.

Thoughts take flight on dandelion seeds,
While squirrels debate on nutty deeds.
Nature chuckles in shades so bright,
Painting the day with sheer delight.

Oh, to ponder in hues so wild,
Becoming once more that playful child.
With every gust, hilarity grows,
What a wacky world this wind bestows!

Glistening Shadows of Aromatic Night

Moonlight drips like honey sweet,
Casting shadows where laughter meets.
Crickets chirp their nightly tune,
While fireflies plot a lighting boon.

The lilies laugh beneath the stars,
Composing songs for passing cars.
Whispers of lavender float about,
Inviting giggles, turning doubt out.

Each scent a clue in the fragrant air,
Mysteries hide behind the fair.
As night unfurls her quirkiness bright,
Everything dances in joyful delight.

With shadows falling, antics ensue,
A party of blooms, oh, who knew?
Eccentric scents lead the way,
To a wild laughter-filled ballet!

Fragrance of Forgotten Lovers

Once upon a time, oh so sweet,
Two hearts met under the summer heat.
With roses red and daisies white,
They danced with shadows on warm, breezy nights.

Their laughter echoed like petals blown,
In a garden where wild things were grown.
Yet now they search for scents long past,
Recalling moments that didn't last.

A whiff of mint brings back that grin,
While wistful thyme makes memories spin.
Basil winks with a knowing stare,
As if to say, don't you dare despair.

In this bouquet of love's old shame,
Each sprig and scent still plays the game.
For even in absence, joy's on the run,
Lovers' fragrances still dance just for fun.

Trails of Whispered Secrets

In the garden, just a whiff,
The roses giggle, what a gift!
Lilies gossip, who's the best?
Tulips chuckle in their nest.

Leaves dance softly in the breeze,
Nature's laughter, what a tease!
Petals blush as bees parade,
Pollination masquerade!

Breezes carry silly tales,
Of skunks and squirrels, epic fails.
A dandelion sneezes loud,
Causing mayhem in the crowd!

Hidden secrets, scents that play,
In this fragrant, joking way.
Nature's humor all around,
In every sniff, joy is found.

The Symphony of Scented Paths

Winding paths of floral notes,
Daisies dance in tiny coats.
A symphony of bright bouquets,
Tickling noses in funny ways.

Breezes whisper, secrets sent,
Mocking flowers, pure content.
Lavender's giggle, mint's sly grin,
In this concert, all join in.

Sunny sunflowers stand so tall,
With popcorn scents, they enthrall.
Marigolds in trumpet flair,
Play a tune that floats through air!

Nature's joke in every breeze,
Scented laughter, sure to please.
Join the dance, don't hold back,
On this fragrant, funny track!

Soft Echoes of Nature's Breath

Whispers flutter, soft and light,
Nature's breath, a pure delight.
Mossy carpets hide some laughs,
Every shrub, a tale that chaffs.

Crickets chirp, a silly tune,
Underneath the winking moon.
Frogs croak jokes of epic fails,
Echoing through the mossy trails.

Tiny bugs in wild ballet,
With every step, they swoop and sway.
Even roots are laughing loud,
In their tangled, merry crowd!

Listen close, their giggles swell,
Nature's secrets, who can tell?
In this world of green and jest,
Laughter whispers at its best.

A Canvas of Aromatic Dreams

Painted blossoms on the rise,
Colors dancing, nature's spies.
Each aroma tells a tale,
Of cheeky winds that never fail.

With a splash of jasmine bright,
And a hint of sheer delight.
Peonies with capes of flair,
Whirl and twirl in scented air.

Lavish layers of perfume,
Filling hearts with sweet consume.
Butterflies are jesters here,
Tickling noses, spreading cheer!

A canvas bright, all scents collide,
Playful notes, they cannot hide.
In this world of fragrant gleam,
Laughter blooms like a sweet dream.

Garden of Wandering Thoughts

In the garden of my brain,
A squirrel debates with a snail,
They argue under the sun,
While I forget what I need to email.

Petunias giggle in the breeze,
The daisies dance in their socks,
A butterfly steals a sneeze,
And I trip over my own thoughts.

The sun dons a silly hat,
As bees throw a party at noon,
I ponder if grass can chat,
While my shoes plot a quick tune.

Lemons laugh on the vine,
Bananas juggle with ease,
The cucumbers sip on wine,
Mercury spins, hoping to please.

Serenity in Bloom

The daisies wear polka dots,
While lilies sport a mustache,
Roses recite funny knots,
In antics, they rather dash.

The sun winks at the cacti,
Who dance in tippy-toe shoes,
While clouds puff out a sigh,
And rain joins in with the blues.

Butterflies take a ballet,
Their pirouettes quite absurd,
As worms cheer from the hay,
And laughter is the main word.

The gardener chuckles a lot,
As tomatoes spin in place,
Each plant, a whimsical thought,
In this veggie-filled embrace.

The Perfumed Pathways

Spices mingle in the air,
With garlic donning a crown,
The pepper shimmies without care,
While I'm lost, about to frown.

Chives whisper secrets low,
Basil jests with a wink,
As I stumble through rows aglow,
In a fragrance I can't think.

The thyme grins, playing a game,
While rosemary's telling tall tales,
Sage rolls in, shouting my name,
As I hunt for the snacks in pails.

Lavender lolls in delight,
Pineapple shares a broad grin,
In this maze, what a sight,
Finding parsley under my chin!

Whispers of the Herbal Night

Mint giggles on a cool breeze,
While chamomile stirs in a pot,
Thyme pulls pranks to appease,
And rosemary's quite the hotshot.

Lemon balm shares a sweet jest,
As shadows play hide and seek,
Cats dance on the herbal crest,
With laughter that's quick and sleek.

The stars sprinkle sage above,
As the night whispers their charms,
In this herbal dream, I love,
While chives throw a party with arms.

The moon chuckles with the night,
Jasmine winks down from its place,
A feast of scents in soft light,
In this garden, joy takes grace.

The Citrus Kiss of Afternoon

In the sun's warm glow, a laugh does bloom,
Lemonade spills, creating joyous room.
Oranges dance with the bees on the wing,
While marmalade jests and giggles do sing.

Ripe in the orchard, a silly parade,
Fruit wearing hats, what treasures we've made!
Grapefruit twirls, it's a zesty delight,
While limes crack jokes, bringing laughter in sight.

Lemons play pranks, jumping from high,
As tangerines roll by, daring to fly.
In the citrusy air, all worries take flight,
And the sweetness of joy makes the world feel right.

Lyrical Notes in Lavender

In fields of purple, the bumblebees hum,
Lavender giggles, a soft, fragrant drum.
Petals fall softly, like whispers that tease,
As butterflies waltz on a warm summer breeze.

The lavender breeze has a funny little scheme,
Making the clouds burst into lavender cream.
Silly little larks sing their lavender tune,
While scattered lavender stars wink at the moon.

A lavender laugh floats above the trees,
Tickling the branches, exciting the bees.
In this whimsical dance, all life is a play,
With lavender dreams brightening the day.

The Breath of Nature's Whisper

Nature chuckles in the rustle of leaves,
As whispers of wind wear ticklish sleeves.
The flowers exchange their murmur delight,
While shadows play hopscotch with beams of light.

Dewdrops giggle as they slide down the stem,
Each tiny droplet a refreshing gem.
The trees tell tales of their roots' silly plight,
While squirrels play tag, a lively sight.

Gentle breezes tease the butterflies' dance,
Creating a symphony, a chance romance.
In the breath of nature, laughter does bloom,
Turning the garden into a grand room.

Crafted in the Essence of Rain

Pitter-patter chorus on rooftops choiring,
Clouds munch popcorn as thunder gets boring.
Raindrops giggle, splashing on the ground,
Each puddle reflects a circus unbound.

The raincoat's a costume, the boots are a joke,
While umbrellas twirl with a weathered yoke.
A drippy parade of cloud-mischeifs deploy,
As nature's laughter brings innocent joy.

Wet socks are the punchline, slipping and sliding,
With laughter echoing, joy multiplying.
In the essence of rain, humor's always in sight,
Crafting smiles worldwide, from morning to night.

Petals and Poetics

In a garden where petals dance,
Bees wear tiny pants, they prance.
Each flower boasts a vibrant hue,
While daisies giggle, laughing too.

Whispers of blooms float in the air,
Sunflowers charm with golden flair.
Tulips tease with a subtle wink,
As mushrooms plot and quietly think.

A rose tells tales of love's sweet jest,
While garlic snickers, never the best.
In this playground of scents so grand,
Nature's comedy, simply unplanned.

So let us frolic in this bloom,
Swaying to the perfume's wild tune.
With petals beneath our playful feet,
Life's a joke, and oh, so sweet!

A Symphony of Scented Hearts

A symphony of smells in the breeze,
Where the lilacs wink, and the roses tease.
Daffodils with their sunny glow,
Say the strangest things you'd never know.

Carnations wearing polka-dot ties,
Make jokes with daisies, oh what a surprise!
Jasmine's laughter fills the cool night air,
While orchids are busy grooming their hair.

With each whiff, the world does sway,
To a fragrant tune that leads astray.
Who knew a sprig could be so grand,
With dreams and giggles playing hand in hand?

So dance to the scent of life's delight,
With petals and giggles, all feels right.
This fragrant ball is quite the feat,
Where every bloom brings laughs, oh sweet!

Inhale the Remnants of Dawn

As dawn breaks with a scent so bright,
I inhale the remnants of the night.
A garlic breath trails like a ghost,
While mint leaves cheer, they love to boast.

Morning glories yawn and stretch,
Each petal opening, the light to fetch.
A daisy snickers, nudging the morn,
"Wake up, sleepyhead, you look quite worn!"

The scent of coffee wafts like a song,
"Join us, dear friend, it won't be long!"
With every sniff, a chuckle shared,
Flavors collide, none are spared.

So inhale deeply, let laughter swell,
In the essence of dawn, we weave our spell.
Every breath a joke, each petal a smile,
In this scented story, let's linger awhile.

Secrets Beneath the Flowering Canopy

Underneath the leafy dome,
Squirrels plot in a fragrant home.
Petals whisper secrets so sly,
While butterflies giggle and flutter by.

The blossoms gossip, pink and bright,
Laughing at bees that take off in flight.
"Did you hear what the fern said today?
About the tulip's dubious bouquet?"

Crickets serenade with a rustling tune,
While violets chuckle beneath the moon.
The garden is alive with sounds of cheer,
As roses blush and throw back a sneer.

In this hidden world, with scents interlace,
Every bloom's a character, every scent has grace.
So let's join the fun in this leafy quest,
Where petals share laughter, and we feel blessed.

Scented Whispers in the Breeze

In the garden, a flower sneezes,
Bees chuckle in blooming breezes.
A daisy wears a polka dot hat,
It looks confused, a playful cat.

The roses gossip with the thyme,
Complaining about the bees' rhyme.
Lavender floats on a silly whim,
While sunflowers sway, looking quite dim.

A jasmine sighs, quite out of tune,
As daisies dance beneath the moon.
Petunias giggle, oh what a scene,
In a world where plants are so keen.

Lemon balm pulls a prank on mint,
Spilling secrets you wouldn't hint.
In this garden, laughter's the aim,
Where scents unite in a funny game.

Aromas of a Silent Dawn

As dawn tiptoes on soft, shy feet,
Pancakes sprout with a syrupy greet.
The coffee pot sings a morning tune,
While waffles dream of maple's boon.

The bread in the toaster starts to sing,
A pop, a dance, what joy does it bring!
While eggs pratfall in a buttery slide,
Each breakfast tale, a whimsical ride.

Outside, the air's filled with giggling dew,
Grass blades whisper, 'We've woke up too!'
A squirrel shares a juicy tale,
With a nutty grin, it starts to wail.

The sun yawns wide, stretching its rays,
Tickling flowers to join in the play.
As morning unfolds with flavors so bright,
In silent giggles, the day takes flight.

Petals on the Pages

In an old book, petals took a seat,
Waiting for words to rhyme with their beat.
Ink spills laughter, stories unfold,
As daisies recite what bees have told.

A rose complains about the yard's mess,
'Who needs weeds?' it says with finesse.
Orchids roll their eyes so lush,
As pages turn, making quite a hush.

Characters jump with a floral twist,
In tales where nothing goes amiss.
A thistle wearing a crown so bright,
Charges boldly, ready for a fight.

Yet all the blooms just laugh and play,
In stories where scents lead the way.
They leap from the pages, wild and free,
In this world, laughter's the key.

Incense of a Dreaming Heart

In a room where dreams like to hide,
A candle flickers, lively and wide.
Chocolates melt with a giggling flair,
As scents of vanilla swirl in the air.

The walls whisper tales of sweet delight,
While shadows dance in the dimming light.
A pillow laughs, wearing a grin,
'This is where the fun begins!'

Jasmine drapes comfortably on a chair,
Sharing secrets, floating on air.
Each laugh lingers like sweet perfume,
As the heart swells, filling the room.

And when the world seems dull and stark,
Light a stick, watch the magic spark.
Let scents collide, stir up a chat,
In a dreaming heart, where laughter's at.

Whispering Violets in a Quiet Night

In the garden of dreams, they giggle,
Yet the moonlight slips, like a shy cat.
Petals whisper secrets, oh so light,
While crickets dance in their little hats.

A curious bee, with a belly so round,
Stumbles and fumbles, all lost in delight.
'What's this?', he hums, 'A dance on the ground?'
But the flowers just laugh at his silly flight.

Tapestry of Essence and Energy

In a world made of scents, oh what a place,
Where lemons wear hats and the mint likes to race.
Elderberry chuckles from way up high,
While lavender winks, sending sighs to the sky.

Cinnamon twirls with a devilish grin,
As nutmeg and ginger join in with a spin.
Together they giggle, concocting a brew,
A potion of fun that smells like a stew.

Breath of the Wind's Bouquet

Oh breeze, you sly trickster, up to your games,
Whispering scents like a child with no aims.
You toss daffodils and let daisies play,
While roses just sigh, 'It's a windy day!'

With every gust comes a giggle or two,
Knocking daises down, saying, 'Who are you?'
Laughter's a breeze, it's all in the air,
Flowers all joining in, without a care.

The Imprint of Fragrance on Memory

Remember that time when we danced with the thyme?
We waltzed through the mint, it felt quite sublime.
Cloves, they were frowning, all out of tune,
While the lilacs just giggled, they knew we'd be doomed.

A whiff of nostalgia, a tickle of laugh,
As jasmine whispers, 'Let's take a photograph!'
Snapshots of scents fill our hearts and our minds,
While we chase after laughter that never unwinds.

Echoes of Geraniums and Dreams

In a garden where the rhymes play,
Geraniums giggle under the sun's ray.
Bees wear tiny hats, oh what a sight,
Pollinating flowers, feeling quite light.

Butterflies dance with whimsical grace,
Chasing their shadows, an elegant race.
A squirrel juggles acorns, the crowd in glee,
Nature's circus, come and see!

The Breath of Nature in Verse

A breeze whispers tales of the tree,
It tickles the leaves, quite carefree.
The flowers gossip in colors so bright,
Spreading laughter from morning to night.

A worm in a top hat winks at a bee,
Saying, "Join me for tea, it's lovely, you'll see!"
While clouds wear their fluffiest costumes,
They float by, chuckling in fun-filled rooms.

Narratives Wrapped in Blossoms

Petunias plot mischief on sunny days,
Sharing secrets in their petal displays.
Laughter erupts from a nearby rose,
Tickling noses as the wind blows.

Daisies debate who is fluffiest here,
Each petal a vote, it's all very clear.
The tulips strut with a floral flair,
Their stories bloom in the crisp, fresh air.

The Elixir of Nature's Hues

Colors clash in a delighted war,
Cabbage leaves laugh from the garden floor.
Sunflowers tilt, wearing crowns of gold,
They wink at the daisies, so fiercely bold.

A cherry tree blushes with fruits that tease,
While ladybugs play tag with the buzzing bees.
In this wild chaos, joy never ends,
Nature's symphony, where mirth transcends.

Aromatic Dreams Take Flight

In a garden of socks, where the daisies smell bold,
Ducks wear sunglasses, all shiny and gold.
Flavors of laughter swirl in the breeze,
As chickens dance tango with flamboyant peas.

Tulips are gossiping, they know all the tea,
While sherbet clouds giggle, all so carefree.
The butterflies waltz in their candy-striped suits,
Making friends with the crickets in funky green boots.

Scented confetti rains down from above,
With the fervor of cake on a day filled with love.
And though it sounds wild, it's simply divine,
A place where the flowers sip sweet lemonade wine.

So let your dreams flutter, and take to the sky,
In this garden of giggles, we learn how to fly.
With aromas of joy, we'll dance through the night,
In a whimsical world where we're all full of light.

The Language of Blossoms

Forget fancy words, just let the blooms chat,
Roses are blushing, while tulips tip their hat.
They whisper sweet secrets in petal-filled tones,
And make jokes about bees and their funny old drones.

Sunflowers grin wide, like a friendly fist pump,
While daisies crack jokes about the neighbor's big dump.
Lilies are giggling, their laughter's a spree,
As they float together on the pond's cup of tea.

Each stem has a story, each leaf sings a song,
In a language of blossoms, where nobody's wrong.
They pollinate puns, with a delicate grace,
Making nature their stage in this colorful place.

So come join the party, the floral delight,
Where petals and pollen have all taken flight.
The humor is timeless, in colors so bright,
In a world where the flowers dance into the night.

Essence of Morning Dew

In the morn, a tale of damp glistening cheer,
Where droplets are giggling, so bright and so clear.
They drip from the leaves, like laughter set free,
In a concert of nature, just you wait and see.

Each blade in the grass plays a fun little tune,
While crickets in bow ties dance under the moon.
The flowers do yoga, stretching their bright hues,
As they sip on the sunshine and skip all the blues.

So grab your best socks, let's waddle on through,
As we laugh with the daisies and feel morning's hue.
For every cool drop is a nose-reddening laugh,
In this playful parade, there's no need for a path.

And as the day warms, and dew starts to fade,
These whimsical moments, together well-made.
With wanders of giggles and bright air to breathe,
The essence of mornings is a joy to believe.

Fragrance in Twilight's Embrace

In twilight's soft arms, the scents start to play,
With perfumes like giggles that dance and sway.
The crickets are crooning their funny serenade,
While the roses shake hands, in a fragrant parade.

Fireflies twinkle like fairies at night,
Jasmine drops puns with an air of delight.
The moon grins down, with a mischievous glance,
As the shadows all join in a twinkling dance.

Lavender bubbles with laughter so sweet,
And dandelions dream of their next tasty treat.
With pollen-filled jokes that they whisper and share,
Underneath a blanket of stars in the air.

So let's join this revel, with noses held high,
As bouquets of mirth laugh and light up the sky.
In twilight's embrace, where the senses ignite,
We find all the humor in the lavender night.

In the Company of Petals

Dancing blooms in the breeze,
They whisper secrets to the bees.
A bouquet wearing a bright smile,
Catching laughter for a while.

Pollen party on a light breeze,
Flower hats and swaying knees.
Bees with ties and floral shoes,
In their garden, nothing to lose.

Petals gossip, scents collide,
In this garden, they all confide.
Throwing petals like confetti,
A blooming circus, oh so witty.

In this patch, no room for gloom,
Every bud has found their room.
With laughter ringing loud and clear,
Who knew flowers had such cheer?

Essence and Kinship of the Evening Sun

The sun bows down with a wink,
As shadows gather 'round to drink.
Golden rays like giggles spread,
A toast to twilight, all misled.

Crickets chirp a silly tune,
Dance beneath the laughing moon.
Sunset's palette spills and splatters,
While fireflies plot their merry patters.

Clouds in pajamas slip away,
Daring night to come out and play.
Scent of humor fills the air,
Tickling noses without a care.

Evening's glow is most absurd,
Like a joke without a word.
All the stars join in the fun,
Under the watch of the cheeky sun.

Aromatic Journeys Through Stillness

In the quiet, scents abound,
With each breath, laughter found.
Minty giggles in the breeze,
Whispers twirling with such ease.

Lavender tickles, oh so sly,
Nose in the air, oh my, oh my!
Each scent a friend, a bold charade,
In this stillness, pranks are played.

Cinnamon sneezes, ginger jives,
Spicy whispers keep it alive.
Every whiff a playful tease,
In calm, we dance with great ease.

A journey through the scents quite grand,
With every laugh, we take a stand.
In quietude, we find our thrill,
Where stillness holds a fragrant chill.

Hues of Scent and Sublime

A whiff of chaos in the air,
Colors clash, a wild affair.
Pink and green in a swirling fight,
Making mischief deep in the night.

A spritz of orange, a splash of blue,
Creating giggles wherever we flew.
Scents of laughter fill the room,
Bubbling chaos, perfume blooms.

Petals play tag with a gust of wind,
Sings of kitchens where fun has sinned.
As tangerine dreams collide with night,
Hues of fragrance keep joy in sight.

In this game of scent and shade,
Every moment, a vibrant parade.
With humor painted wide and free,
In hues of laughter, we find glee.

Threading Through Blossom-Laden Paths

In gardens bright, we roam and play,
With petals soft and paths that sway.
A bee buzzes by with mischief in flight,
While tulips giggle, a comical sight.

The daisies dance, their rhythm so grand,
As if to say, "Come join our band!"
A squirrel swoops down, quite sly and spry,
Chasing his tail while the flowers sigh.

With each step taken, a flower winks,
They plot and scheme, or so it thinks.
A puppy rolls in the dandelion dust,
His nose all yellow, oh what a fuss!

So we laugh and skip, with petals above,
In this fragrant world, we share our love.
To thread these paths, to twirl and prance,
Is a joyous ode to the plant-life dance.

Where Wildflowers Speak

Among the wilds, they gather and grin,
A chorus of colors, but whose joke is in?
The buttercup whispers, 'I'm all that you need,'
While laughing at roses for being so seed.

The sunflowers tower with a wink and a smile,
'Just look at us, we are quite the style!'
While clover chuckles in patches of green,
'Where'd you find those pants? They're quite the scene!'

The violets gossip with tales of the breeze,
'He tickles our petals, oh what a tease!'
And daisies nod, joining in on the fun,
They throw little parties, 'til the day is done.

So if you wander where wild blooms reside,
You'll hear their whispers, their giggles, their pride.
In this curious patch, where laughter is found,
The flowers unite, a comedic surround.

The Unseen Threads of Scent

There's a mystery here, an invisible line,
Woven by petals, oh how divine!
The air is a canvas, painted bright and bold,
With every fragrance, a story is told.

The mint makes a joke about thyme getting old,
While lavender giggles, her perfume unfolds.
Cinnamon chuckles, a pinch here and there,
'Are you sweet or savory? Oh, who really cares?'

The jasmine murmurs, 'Are we all just a whims?'
While citrus provides a zing to the hymns.
Then basil pipes up, 'Let's all have a feast!'
'With olfactory delights, we'll party at least!'

So let's weave our noses, together we'll find,
These threads of aroma, so quirky and kind.
In this fragrant tapestry, humor will bloom,
With scents of delight that will brighten the room.

A Haven of Herbal Serendipity

In a garden of herbs where the laughter is bright,
Basil tells tales, each one a delight.
Thyme cracks a pun, as rosemary snorts,
While sage shakes his head, 'You two are all sorts!'

The mint sprigs jump with a zing in the air,
'Let's brew up some tea, if you all dare!'
Then chamomile yawns, 'I'll just take a nap,'
While sage looks perplexed, like 'What's her gap?'

In this herbal haven, the jokes don't run dry,
As oregano shares secrets, oh me, oh my!
Parsley just giggles, adding some zest,
'Can we stir up trouble? Oh, that would be best!'

So let's brew together, in pots large and small,
In this quirky garden, there's room for us all.
With scents swirling 'round, in a culinary twist,
A haven of laughter, in every herb, we persist.

Fragrant Footnotes of Existence

In the garden of silence, a bee sneezes,
Dusting off petals, he never ceases.
A dandelion laughs, wearing a crown,
While a sunflower grins, never a frown.

The roses gossip about their perfume,
While daisies dance in a glorious bloom.
A tulip trips over a bright green shoe,
And the violets chuckle at the sky so blue.

With a waft of clumsiness in the air,
The lilies giggle in their fragrant lair.
Petals take notes on what flowers say,
A bloom-filled lecture, in a quirky way.

Each scent a story, each laugh a cheer,
In a garden where absurdity draws near.
The world is a stage with flowers as cast,
In the play of aromas, a riotous blast.

Love Letters to the Blooming World

A daisy scribbles notes on the breeze,
Telling tales of love to bumblebee peas.
Petals whisper sweet nothings at dawn,
While a ladybug blushes, her shyness all gone.

The tulips write poems in colors so bright,
Sending sunbeams as kisses, pure delight.
Each rose has a crush on the morning sun,
In a world full of scents, where laughter is spun.

The wind plays a trick, tickling the trees,
As flowers giggle under the buzzing bees.
Every scent a confession, with puns on the side,
In this love-letter garden, we laugh and abide.

The blossoms exchange glances, a wink and a nod,
In a silly romance where the earth is a prod.
Their sweet little secrets slip out with a sigh,
As they aroma-mingle beneath the sky.

The Harmony of a Jasmine Sunset

As the sun dips low, with a wink and a flash,
The jasmine giggles, in a soft, rosy sash.
With scents that tickle and pirouette too,
The sky is a canvas of bright colored dew.

Crickets compose symphonies, chirps in the night,
While shadows and scents dance in pure delight.
A cloud takes a bow, just before it departs,
And every note carries a tickle to hearts.

The moon joins the party, with silver so shy,
Casting smiles on petals as they wave goodbye.
Each fragrance a note in this fragrant ballet,
Where night blooms awaken in a cheeky display.

Laughter paints stars in the whispering dark,
As jasmine scents twirl, a whimsical spark.
In harmony's glow, we find our sweet bliss,
In this joking serenade, not one soul can miss.

Scented Solitude

In a corner of quiet, the lavender sighs,
While the sage tells tall tales that float to the skies.
A single rose broods, reflecting on days,
Of friendships with daisies and their silly ways.

The thyme has a moment, with thoughts all alone,
Making up jokes with a sweet undertone.
While the lilacs roll laughter, like marbles on air,
In this fragrant retreat, there's humor to share.

In the stillness of scent, where laughter can bloom,
A pinecone joins in, as the chill starts to loom.
With each waft of humor, the quiet grows bright,
Making solitude sing in the soft, gentle night.

So let each lone flower in fragrance unfurl,
Finding joy in the quiet, this whimsical whirl.
In scented seclusion, where chuckles entwine,
We discover that laughter can flourish, divine.

The Language of Blooming Hearts

In gardens where giggles grow,
Petals whisper jokes on the breeze,
Bumblebees dance with silly flow,
While daisies nod in playful tease.

Sunflowers strut with sunshine hats,
Tulips do the cha-cha in line,
Laughter spills like spilled sweet sprats,
As roses waltz in a twist of vine.

The violets chuckle at their bling,
With laughter wrapped in scent so bold,
A floral chorus begins to sing,
As hearts bloom bright, stories unfold.

So let's sip the nectar of cheer,
In our floral frolics, joy will meet,
With petals bright, and no need for fear,
Dance with the blooms, feel the sweet heat.

Resonance of Perfumed Moments

A whiff of whimsy fills the air,
Jasmine jokes, and lilac laughs,
In every corner, scents declare,
Fragrance has its playful gaffes.

Chocolates in the rose garden tease,
Where mint leaves giggle at the rain,
Even pine cones chuckle in the breeze,
Each note brings forth a comical strain.

Dandelions puff out loud and clear,
"Blow us, make a wish!" they cry,
While lavender's delicate veneer,
Whispers sweet nothings as time slips by.

So capture each moment, let it spin,
In this scent-filled rhapsody of glee,
For the joy in bouquet's spin,
Is in laughter shared, wild and free.

The Aroma of Dusk's Embrace

As twilight drapes a colorful shawl,
Clover giggles in the fading light,
With evening scents that begin to sprawl,
Chasing shadows, evoking delight.

Candles flicker, like fireflies shy,
As chamomile winks with soft appeal,
While young ferns crave a midnight sigh,
And mint dreams of a sprightly wheel.

The night unfolds its scented tales,
With every bloom holding a jest,
As roses tease with fragrant trails,
Dusk's embrace becomes a zestful quest.

So let the aroma tickle your nose,
And pulse like a rhythm in your heart,
For within this dusk, the laughter grows,
In every scent, a funny part.

Whiffs of Color and Emotion

In the garden where colors collide,
Tulips tumble in colorful cheer,
Every hue takes a comical slide,
As laughter blossoms like springtime beer.

Cactus joins in with sharp wit and charm,
While daisies spin tales of delight,
With petals that spill fun without harm,
Creating a ruckus in soft moonlight.

Morning glories giggle at dawn,
Butterflies flutter in giggly flight,
Echoes of smiles in bright lawns,
Awaken joy in the daylight's light.

So twirl in the scents and hues so bold,
In this vibrant, amusing display,
Each whiff brings stories of laughter told,
A bouquet of fun in the sun's warm sway.

The Tang of Earth and Sky

The clouds wore socks, oh what a sight,
A rainbow slipped on, feeling quite bright.
The sun danced with the trees in glee,
While squirrels laughed, so cheekily.

Pine cones rolled like bowling balls,
While dandelions played with their falls.
The breeze tickled the bumblebee's wings,
As nature burst forth in mischievous springs.

Giraffes wore hats, slightly askew,
As elephants splashed in shade of blue.
A chase of shadows around the hill,
Made the day's laughter louder still.

In the sky a kite took a dive,
Chasing clouds, feeling so alive.
With each twist and turn, giggles abound,
In the tang of earth, joy's rarely found.

A Diary Inked in Petals

Petals scribble secrets on a breeze,
Daisies gossip under shady trees.
Each bloom a story, wild and bright,
Whispering tales of night and light.

Tulips wear pajamas, pink and blue,
Laughing with lilies, 'Come dance, would you?'
The roses sigh, they've heard it all,
While violets shyly blush and sprawl.

Butterflies tweeting, tops of their lungs,
With beetles tapping out silly songs.
In this grassy diary, laughter flows,
Ink made of sunshine, joy that glows.

A breeze turns the pages, flapping with glee,
Each flower a letter, a giggling spree.
With every petal that flits and sways,
Imagination writes through funny days.

Moonlit Gardens of Imagination

In gardens where the stars wear crowns,
Moonbeams play hopscotch on silver towns.
Pansies chuckle, tickling the night,
As fireflies join in with their bright light.

A cat in a bow tie chats with the moon,
While crickets compose an odd little tune.
Naps are taken by hedgehogs nearby,
As owls give wisdom to those who try.

Sunflowers dream of waltzing with stars,
While snails zoom by, leaving tiny scars.
The night hums a tune of playful delight,
In moonlit gardens, everything feels right.

Ideas blossom like blooms in full bloom,
With laughter that lingers, chasing the gloom.
With each twinkle and giggle, night finds its way,
In gardens of laughter, forever we play.

Olfactories of Time's Passage

Time tiptoes softly, socks on its feet,
With scents that giggle, oh how sweet!
Clocks tickle noses with a whiff of cheer,
As moments unfold, tickling here and there.

The coffee spills secrets, warm and bright,
While muffins conspire in morning light.
Each whiff a joke, a laugh to share,
As butter croissants float without a care.

Baking bread dreams of crusty delight,
As cinnamon rolls join in the fight.
A sprinkle of sugar makes stories sweet,
In the olfactories where time takes a seat.

So let every scent hum its funny rhyme,
As we dance through the hours, wrapped in time.
A world full of fragrances makes spirits rise,
In this merry symphony, everyone sighs.

Entwined in Floral Composition

In a garden where tigers are bright,
A duck wears a hat, oh what a sight!
Tulips giggle as daisies dance,
Together they weave a floral romance.

Bumblebees hum an offbeat tune,
A rose blushes beneath the moon.
Worms don tuxedos, ready to sway,
While daisies debate, 'Who leads the ballet?'

Laughter echoes through the green maze,
As vines get tangled in silly ways.
A sunflower pranks with a cheeky grin,
And all the petunias shout, 'Let's begin!'

So join the twirl, in petals deep,
Where giggles and fragrances slowly seep.
In this humorous plot, let's explode,
Amongst blooms where fun is bestowed.

Reverberations of Sweet Petals

There once was a blooming ol' thyme,
Who swore it could rap in perfect rhyme.
It rattled leaves, puffs of air,
While marigolds snickered, unaware.

Floral jokes wafted through the air,
'Why did the daisy take a dare?'
'To prove it was bright and not just pretty!'
Such petals of humor, oh so witty!

A cactus joins in, feeling kind,
With prickly puns, oh he's one of a kind!
Petals burst out in giggling fits,
As they belly-laugh through virtual bits.

In this amusing garden of cheer,
Every bloom has its own funny sphere.
So when life gets too thorny, take note,
Breathe in the humor, let laughter float.

Capturing Moments in Aromatic Lines

The lilac spills tales on a sunny day,
With daisies declaring a grand bouquet.
Stalks intertwined like gossiping friends,
Sharing their breezy, floral blends.

With bees in a tizzy and butterflies bold,
A cloud of zest in stories untold.
Each petal a punchline, ready to share,
As orchids wear spectacles, twinkle, and stare.

Sunflowers whisper, 'What's the catch?'
While roses pose, as if in a match.
The tulips pass notes, filled with glee,
In this aromatic comedy spree!

Fading into twilight, the laughter stays,
Through fragrant reminders of sunny days.
So gather 'round blooms, in humor we trust,
In nature's embrace, we sparkle and rust.

The Dream Weavers of Aroma

In the twilight bloom of lavender skies,
Petals invent pranks, to no one's surprise.
'Knock knock,' says the zesty old sage,
'Who's there?' replies the mint onstage.

With echoes of daisies, the punchlines fly,
As violets fold up with a dramatic sigh.
Where geraniums giggle just to be seen,
And pansies pose in a comedy scene.

A rogue lilac steals the show,
In a jester's cap, with much pomp and flow.
Laughter erupts in this floral embrace,
Where every petal has a quirky face.

So let the blossoms weave dreams anew,
Filling the air with mischief and hue.
Join in the laughter, let petals collide,
In this fragrant fiesta, where joy can't hide.

Olfactory Echoes of Memory

In the kitchen, cookies bake,
Jokes arise, laughter wakes.
A whiff of garlic causes a grin,
How do we fit all this in?

Remember the shoes left by the door?
Scents of socks, we can't ignore.
Each aroma has a tale to spin,
Who knew that shoes could cause such din?

Nostalgic hints from distant pies,
Grandma's hugs and butter flies.
A whiff of lemons, dreamers wake,
Who knew memory could bake?

The air is heavy, yet light and sweet,
With floating giggles, a merry feat.
Each breath a joke, a wink, a tease,
Carried on breezes, flying with ease.

The Bouquet of Untold Stories

Herbs and spices whisper secrets forth,
A truth is told from the south and north.
Pasta recalls that summer rain,
Mixed with laughter, it drowns out the pain.

Onions cry, then swiftly sauté,
As basil dances in a cheeky ballet.
The kitchen spills tales, some loud, some meek,
Al dente dreams, rustling unique.

Aromas twist like fortune's wheel,
Old socks and sunshine, surreal surreal.
In every nook, a memory hides,
Seeking fragrance where humor abides.

Chopping chives, slicing bread,
A laugh comes alive, while butter's spread.
Who knew a whiff could tell a joke?
The bouquet blooms, as laughter chokes.

Scents of Solitude and Sound

A single sandalwood, all alone,
Whispers softly, like a distant tone.
Tea brews quietly, lost among dreams,
Spilling stories from steaming seams.

A crooked chair with echoed sighs,
Melancholy meets to tease the skies.
Incense twirls to an old tune,
Whimsical and cheeky like a opportune.

Lonely socks still smile at night,
Each has a tale that takes flight.
A bouquet of solitude, veiled and shy,
One whiff and they're off into the sky.

An empty room where echoes sleep,
Bottle it up, let secrets creep.
With every scent a flicker goes,
A chorus of laughter, who knows?

A Garden of Unwritten Thoughts

In the garden, ideas bloom,
Petals collide in a scented room.
Mint whispers jokes as bees buzz along,
Creating a melody's fragrant song.

Celery crunches underfoot's tread,
Nature laughs, and so should we, instead.
Each stalk a scribe with tales to tell,
Of fennel dreams that danced so well.

A breeze carries perfume of yesteryear,
With laughter sprouting, let's all cheer!
Pumpkins giggle as they take the stage,
A patchwork of scents on a colorful page.

Behold the herbs that plot and scheme,
Painted by scents in an aromatic dream.
In this garden spun from scents of thought,
Each laugh a blossom, each sigh a plot.

The Veil of Earthy Chords

In a world where muddy shoes dance,
Kicking dirt and laughter in a trance,
A symphony of worms burrowed deep,
While beetles join in, with secrets to keep.

Banjos strum with twang and glee,
As daisies nod in harmony,
A butterfly wobbles on its flight,
Chasing the melodies through the night.

Drifting scents of soil and jest,
Ants march by, feeling quite blessed,
With picnic crumbs and crumbs of cheer,
Belly laughs echo, ringing near.

A chorus of frogs starts a song,
As nature hums the whole night long,
From roots to leaves, it's all a show,
With each earthy chord, the rhythms grow.

Reflections in the Garden's Heart

In a pot filled with giggles and thyme,
Tomato plants sway, keeping time,
A worm in sunglasses slips on by,
To check out the daisies, oh my my!

Sunflowers wear hats, quite dapper,
While beans twist and turn, a funky rapper,
The cucumber's smile is quite worth a glance,
With radishes joining the silly dance.

Rose bushes gossip, whispering low,
About a squirrel with an acorn grow,
The lilies chuckle, a watery jest,
As bees buzz in with a golden zest.

Reflections ripple in the garden's bowl,
Where every bloom plays a vibrant role,
Nature's orchestra strikes up a tune,
As laughter and petals scatter like June.

Nectar of Spoken Words

In the jungle of chatter, words take flight,
Where honeybees sip on stories at night,
A power of puns drips like sweet treats,
As giraffes giggle and share their feats.

A parrot squawks in rhythmic delight,
Telling tales of a cat's odd plight,
With each twist and turn, it brings out the fun,
As laughter bursts bright like a morning sun.

In this buzzing world filled with mirth,
A worm does stand-up, proving its worth,
It wiggles and jigs under the moon's glow,
While crickets applaud the show from below.

Words drip like nectar, sweet and spry,
Crafting a feast for the ear and the eye,
With whispers of joy that tug at the heart,
In this garden of gibberish, we all play our part.

The Essence Between the Lines

Beneath the ink, where secrets lie,
A mischievous comma opens its eye,
It dances like a cat on a string,
While exclamation marks begin to sing.

Paragraphs chuckle, their stories entwined,
With puns that pop like bubbles, defined,
Sentences twirl in a grammar ballet,
As specks of joy float, come what may.

In a realm of quotes that jump off the page,
Where thoughts form a circus, a vibrant stage,
Each line a delight, a humorous spin,
Inviting all readers to join in the din.

This essence of written, alive with surprise,
Winks from the margins, a playful disguise,
For between every line, a joke might reside,
In the whimsical world where words abide.

Beneath the Canopy of Smell

Underneath the trees, a scent does play,
It tickles my nose, makes me sway.
A whiff of pine, oh what a tease,
While bees buzz by, seeking sweet cheese.

A garlic breeze drifts through the park,
I sniff it deep, it hits the mark.
A clash of herbs does spark a grin,
How can a smell bring so much spin?

With every step, a trail I chase,
A waft of cake puts me in place.
I dream of frosting, thick and proud,
While macarons dance, all merry and loud.

Beneath the canopy, I concoct,
Recipes based on the scents I've stroked.
A giggle, a snort, as flavors collide,
In this fragrant realm, I take great pride.

Sweet Notes in the Silence

In the hush of night, a cookie scent,
Makes me wonder where the calories went.
Oh, silence bites while the pastries shout,
Each sweet note puts the diet out.

A chocolate whiff floats through the air,
Followed by laughter, but who really cares?
The fridge hums softly like a lullaby,
Whispers secrets, making me sigh.

If muffins could dance, they'd shimmy and shake,
Until I devour each crumb and brake.
In silence they sing, a sugary song,
Galettes giggle and say, "Come along!"

So here I sit, in the quiet delight,
With dreams of pastries that soar like a kite.
Sweet notes surround me, they tease and jest,
In the silence, it's really the best.

The Elusive Dance of Aroma and Emotion

A whiff of cinnamon, a memory sparks,
Of lazy Sundays and wild shark parks.
With every sniff, I'm lost in delight,
While my coffee winks in the morning light.

Is that a hint of rosemary too?
Reminds me of dinner—oh what a stew!
The dance of garlic, so bold, so bright,
Makes my taste buds ready to take flight.

I see emotions twirling in the air,
Chasing each ghost, I've lost my flair.
Mint and lemon with a pinch of zest,
Bring laughter and joy that I love best.

The dance goes on, through the kitchen and hall,
As aromas weave in this grand ol' ball.
Each scent tells a story, a tale or a pun,
Where laughter and flavors blend into one.

Spice Trails in the Twilight

The sun dips low, spices start to sing,
A trail of cumin makes my heart swing.
In twilight hours, with a sprinkle here,
I follow the scent, for snacks persevere.

A bay leaf beckons, a hint of the night,
It winks at me softly, all playful and bright.
Paprika pirouettes on a breeze so free,
While chili giggles, daring me to flee.

Saffron whispers secrets that shimmer and glow,
As I chase the aroma like a curious crow.
Dancing through shadows, the spices unite,
Creating a banquet in fading daylight.

With each savory step, I twirl with glee,
The spices and I, such a comical spree.
In twilight's embrace, we laugh and we play,
On this fragrant journey, we'll stew the day away.

Where Fragrances and Shadows Play

In the garden where aromas dance,
A bee in a tuxedo breaks out in prance.
Pollen's the confetti of nature's parade,
A rose yells, "I'm fabulous!" while the daisies fade.

Sunbeams tease flowers with unyielding light,
While tulips play tag, oh what a sight!
The daisies keep giggling, they can't get enough,
As lilacs whisper secrets, a little too tough.

A chocolate scent wafts from a nearby treat,
Laughter erupts, joyfully sweet.
The wind tells a joke, in jest it will sway,
As shadows indulge in this light-hearted play.

Thus blossoms and breezes join in the fun,
A party of scents, all basking in sun.
So grab your bouquet, come join in the fray,
Where fragrances twirl and shadows don't stay.

An Ode to the Sunkissed Air

Oh, how the beams tickle roses so bright,
While fireflies giggle at the edge of the night.
The breeze gives a nudge to a daffodil's head,
"Watch out, here comes sun, don't hide in your bed!"

The sunflowers salute, with faces that cheer,
As daisies chime in, in voices so clear.
A frog croaks a ditty, an oafish refrain,
"Join in, my friends, let's bask in the gain!"

In the midst of the laughter, the daisies conspire,
A prank on a flower that just can't retire.
With a blossom on his head, what glamour he'll find,
As the crowd erupts, oh, they're terribly kind!

So here's to the air, the warmth, and the jest,
Where sunflowers sparkle and all feel their best.
Let the laughter resound, as we sway without care,
In this joyous abode of the sunkissed air.

Petals Whisper Softly

In a garden where petals perform little dances,
A butterfly slips, in comical prances.
"Excuse me, dear tulip," it giggles and hums,
"I'm late for a meeting, those flowers are bums!"

Petals drop secrets, like tiny balloons,
As violets share tales beneath glowing moons.
"Oh, did you hear? A bee stole my shade,
But watch how I blossom—I'm never afraid."

The lilies all chuckle, they hold nothing back,
A dandelion grins, looking for a snack.
"Let's blow all our worries away in one breath,
And sow all our laughter, till there's nothing left!"

While shadows creep softly with giggles that blend,
The flowers compete for the title of friend.
In this quirky patch where the humor can't cease,
Petals whisper softly, spreading laughter and peace.

Scented Echoes in the Breeze

Oh, the echoes of scents bubble up with delight,
As the roses keep joking, their petals in flight.
"Who wore it best?" cries a boisterous bloom,
As the lilacs wink and the garden's in bloom.

The air's mixed with laughter and tickles galore,
As a clumsy old bumblebee stumbles once more.
"Mind the curtains, I dance!" comes a chirpy old sprout,
But with dad jokes of nature, he always will pout.

Whispers of mint tease the lavender's feet,
While orange zest challenges the jasmine so sweet.
Each scent tells a story, in giggles, they weave,
In this fragrant ballet, it's hard to believe!

So let's laugh with the petals and sway in the air,
With scented echoes, there's merriment to spare.
In this fragrant escapade, come join and be free,
For giggles are plenty, as wide as the sea.

www.ingramcontent.com/pod-product-compliance
Ingram Content Group UK Ltd.
Pitfield, Milton Keynes, MK11 3LW, UK
UKHW021344170125
4163UKWH00021B/395